NEW IDEAS WITH
DOUGH

A WARD LOCK BOOK

First published in the UK 1996
by Ward Lock
Wellington House
125 Strand
LONDON
WC2R 0BB

A Cassell Imprint

Copyright   © RCS Libri & Grandi Opere S.p.A. Milan 1995
             © English language edition Ward Lock 1996

Distributed in the United States
by Sterling Publishing Co., Inc.
387 Park Avenue South, New York, NY 10016-8810

Distributed in Australia
by Capricorn Link (Australia) Pty Ltd
2/13 Carrington Road, Castle Hill NSW 2154

A British Library Cataloguing in Publication Data block for this book may be obtained from the British Library.

ISBN 0 7063 7565 3
Typeset by G&G computer graphic
Printed and bound in Italy

R. IMOTI

NEW IDEAS WITH
DOUGH

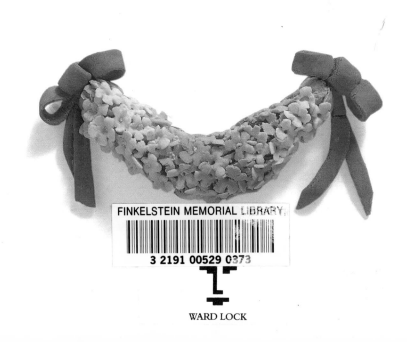

WARD LOCK

CONTENTS

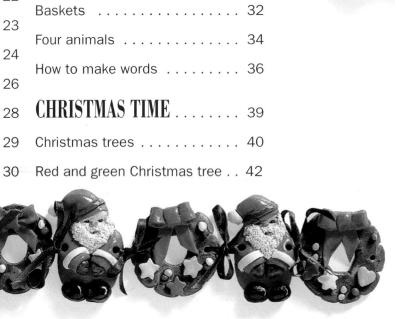

INTRODUCTION

When I was asked to write this salt dough book I panicked. I was not at all prepared for the unexpected success of my first book, in which I thought I had said and done everything possible. I asked for a little time before responding because, of course, I knew I would agree. In fact, I was already missing my workshop kitchen table full of flour and salt, paints, cutters and all my tools. It was here that a thousand little objects took shape inspired perhaps by an illustration, a story, a feeling, an occasion all just waiting to come to life in this book. And so, here I am with page after page of new ideas for you to try out. The techniques are not hard to master. All you need is flour, salt, water and the desire to play, to become a child again, plunging your hands into this soft, warm, malleable material and creating simple pretty shapes: a heart, a piece of fruit, a bunny or a little animal, small, specially-made gifts that are full of magic.

ROSMUNDA IMOTI

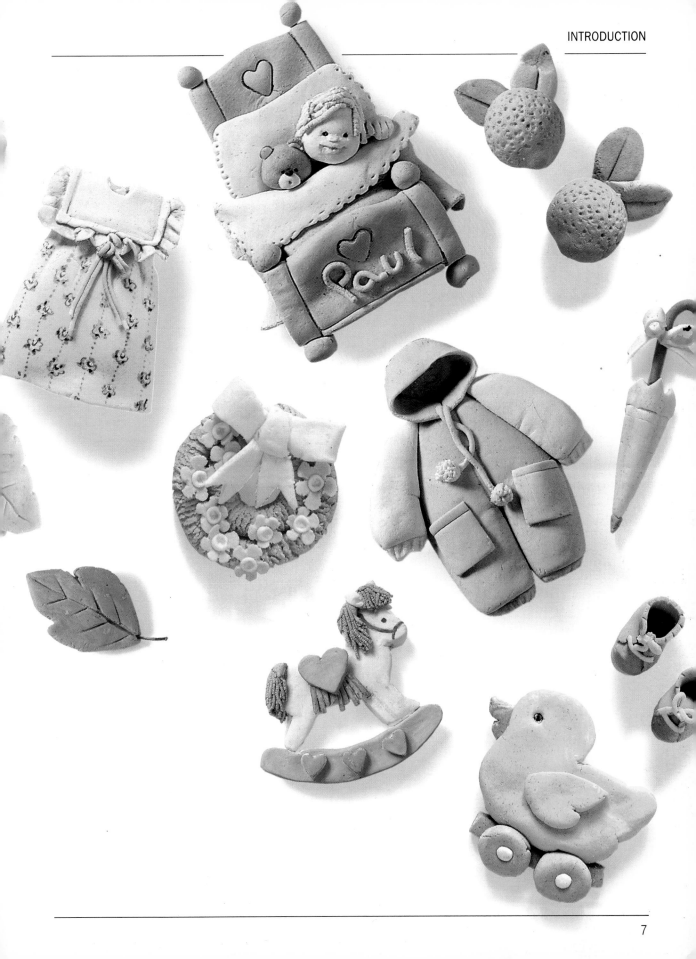

MAKING SALT DOUGH

TOOLS

Simple kitchen utensils are all you need for successful salt dough shapes. With the grater you can make decorative imprints; a rolling pin can be used to produce smooth, even sheets of dough; a garlic press with small holes will produce perfect hair for figures, while one with larger holes will produce thicker strands for writing names in dough. Pastry cutters are ideal for beginners; while a specialist pastry cutter will make neat cuts. Skewers and toothpicks are indispensable, as are wire hooks for hanging the finished pieces. You will also need paint and paintbrushes for finishing off your work.

INGREDIENTS

The essential ingredients for making salt dough are:
- plain white flour
- fine kitchen salt (can be ground in a coffee grinder)
- water at room temperature
You can add the following ingredients to your salt dough to improve the malleability and durability of your projects: wallpaper glue in powder form, glycerine and cooking oil in small amounts.

You can create special colours by using other types of flour and/or adding spices which act as natural dyes. Here are different combinations. From left to right: white flour and finely ground salt, white flour and coarsely ground salt, whole wheat flour, cocoa, rye flour, cinnamon, instant, ground coffee, saffron, curry powder and paprika.

MAKING AND MODELLING THE DOUGH

Here is a good basic dough recipe:

- 200g/7oz of fine salt
- 200g/7oz of plain white flour
- 125ml/4 $\frac{1}{2}$ fl oz of water

Or without exact weights:

- 1 cup of fine salt
- 2 cups of plain white flour
- $\frac{1}{2}$ cup of water

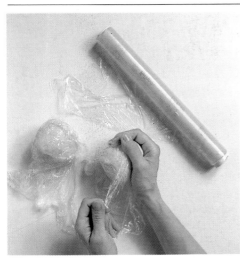

Mix the salt and flour in a large bowl and then add the water. Knead the mixture vigorously until it becomes smooth and elastic. Letting the dough sit for a while before use will improve it. Once made, the dough will last for up to a week if you keep it wrapped in cellophane wrap and stored in a cool place. However do not keep it in the refrigerator. If you plan on baking your piece it's best to work directly on a baking sheet or aluminium foil. Remove the piece from the foil as soon as possible because foil prevents drying. Mould the different elements of your finished piece separately and stick them to each other by brushing with water and gently pressing them together. If the dough dries out while working, just re-knead it with damp hands. If the dough becomes too soft just add a little flour to the mixture.

BAKING AND DRYING

Coloured pieces should be dried and not baked because baking will alter the colour. A radiator is the perfect place to dry your projects. Oven baking requires attention and accurate temperature control. The pieces should be baked at a low temperature, 70°C/158°F or 80°C/176°F for a good half hour and then you can raise the temperature slowly to 90°C/194°F to 100°C/212°F until there is unified colour over the whole piece. Raise the temperature to 180°C/356°F to create the golden colour of bread. The total baking time should be at least two hours though there will be some variation, depending on your oven.

ADDING GLOSS AND FINISH

Once your piece is finished and completely dry, sand it carefully with an emery board or fine grade sandpaper to remove any little imperfections. The smooth surface must then be coated with a protective varnish, gloss or matt, depending on your taste. Brightly coloured pieces look even more vibrant with a glossy finish while muted, neutral colours are more suited to a matt finish. It's important to varnish the whole piece, including the underside, to avoid any intake of moisture. Unvarnished items will not last long.

COLOURING THE DOUGH

You can colour your dough by adding a little bit of paint to the dough mixture. Wearing protective gloves knead the dough until the colour is uniform throughout. You can wrap up your coloured dough in cellophane wrap and then use it as it is or mix it with other coloured dough.

PAINTING
A FINISHED PIECE

Decorating a piece needs some care and you will want to experiment with different paints and brushes. The piece must be totally dry or baked before painting. Remember that paint will make the finished article heavier and will also cover up the natural grain of the dough.

FLOWERS

To make a daisy flatten out a strip of dough and serrate it, forming petals on one side with a toothpick. Curl the strip into a cone and tease out the petals. Make the centre of the flower by putting some dough through a garlic press and arrange the little pieces in the middle of the petals.

The forget-me-not is an easy flower to make. Simply form a ball, flatten it and shape the petals and centre with a toothpick.

To make a primrose form a little salt dough cone on the end of a pencil and then cut the petals out with a pair of small scissors.

A violet is made by forming five distinct petals; the three top ones are longer and thinner while the two bottom petals are more rounded.

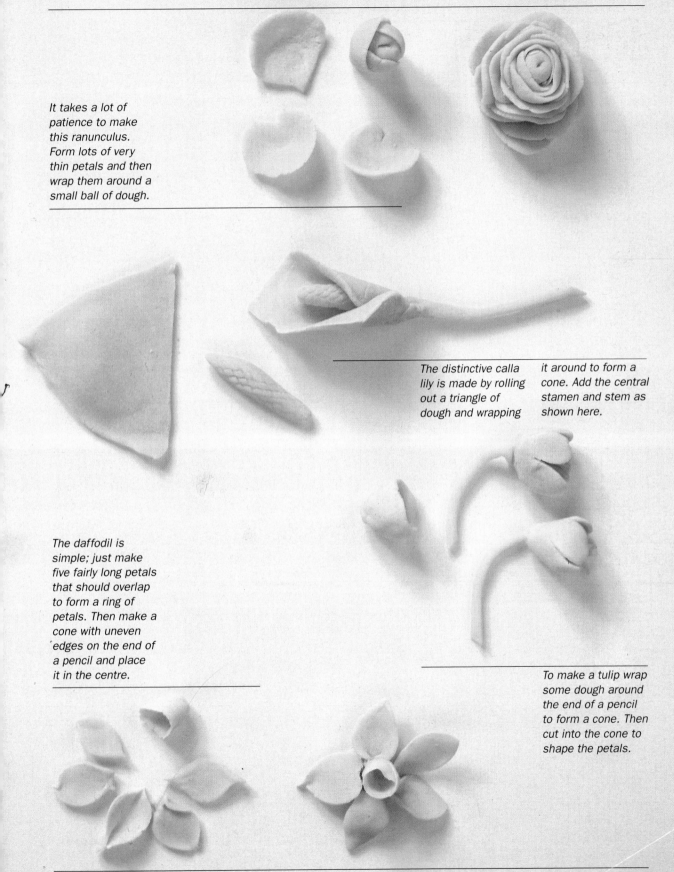

It takes a lot of patience to make this ranunculus. Form lots of very thin petals and then wrap them around a small ball of dough.

The distinctive calla lily is made by rolling out a triangle of dough and wrapping it around to form a cone. Add the central stamen and stem as shown here.

The daffodil is simple; just make five fairly long petals that should overlap to form a ring of petals. Then make a cone with uneven edges on the end of a pencil and place it in the centre.

To make a tulip wrap some dough around the end of a pencil to form a cone. Then cut into the cone to shape the petals.

ROSES

Take special care with your roses because they will add so much to any salt dough project. Here is a way of making a rose with open petals. The key is to have smooth, elastic dough to make really thin petals.

Another type of rose is formed by preparing a cone of dough with a rounded tip. Flatten two strips, wrap them around the tip of the cone and squeeze the bottom to open the petals.

Now add more petals around it and cut just beneath the rose.

VEGETABLES

To make a head of lettuce mould a ball of dough and wrap thin roselike petals with uneven edges around it.

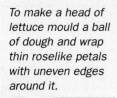

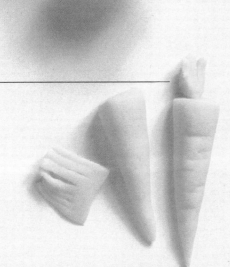

A carrot can be made by moulding a long cone, then indent some horizontal lines on the side and add another piece that is cut into strips on one side to make the carrot top.

The head of the cauliflower is made by pressing dough through a garlic press and then sticking the bits to the top of a dough ball. Then surround the ball with thin but uneven leaves.

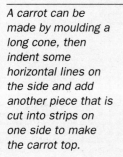

To make a pepper mould a cylinder of dough with rounded edges and use a toothpick to make depressions in the sides. Finish off the top by adding the stalk of a chilli pepper.

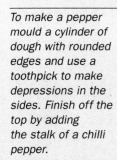

Asparagus is easily made by rolling longish cylinders and making scissors cuts on one end.

FRUIT

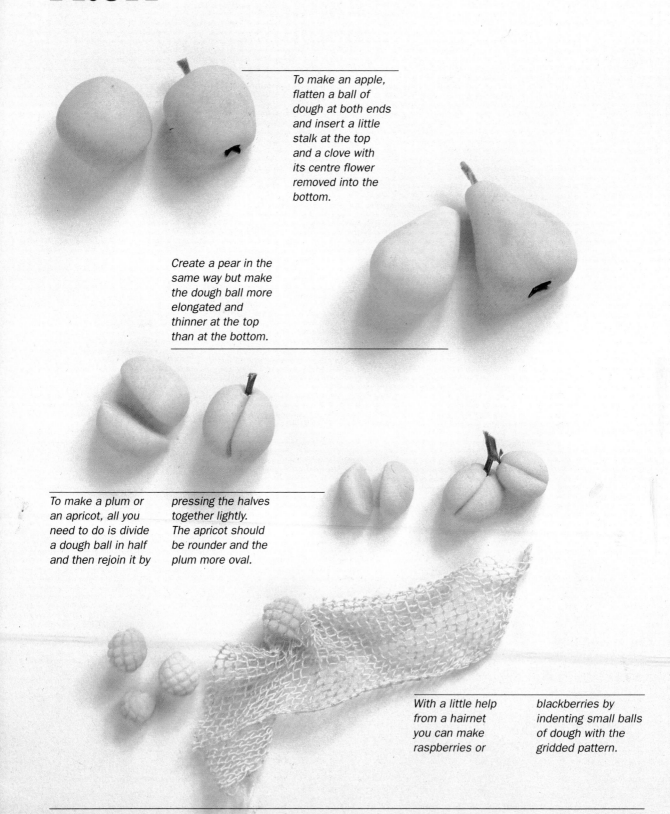

To make an apple, flatten a ball of dough at both ends and insert a little stalk at the top and a clove with its centre flower removed into the bottom.

Create a pear in the same way but make the dough ball more elongated and thinner at the top than at the bottom.

To make a plum or an apricot, all you need to do is divide a dough ball in half and then rejoin it by pressing the halves together lightly. The apricot should be rounder and the plum more oval.

With a little help from a hairnet you can make raspberries or blackberries by indenting small balls of dough with the gridded pattern.

The perfect skin on this pineapple is achieved using wire mesh to indent the pattern.

Oranges and lemons are also rolled over a grater to obtain the necessary rough finish.

To make the dimpled effect on a straw-berry you will need to use the smallest grid of a cheese grater.

To make a bunch of grapes roll a lot of little irregularly shaped balls and form them into a bunch. Add some leaves and make a stem by rolling a thread of dough around a toothpick. Assemble and add a real twig.

LEAVES

Press a small quantity of dough on to a flat surface, make a long leaf shape and use a skewer or toothpick to serrate the edges from the outside inwards. Then press a thin knife onto the dough to create veins.

There is an infinite variety of leaves but the technique for making them is always the same and you will get the best results by using a pastry cutter.

The perfect leaf is best made by making an impression on to the dough with a real leaf. Using a rolling pin and a good amount of dough roll out a piece about $2mm/\frac{1}{8}$ in thick. Put the real leaf on top and cover it with a sheet of plastic and roll over it with the rolling pin.

Then cut the leaf out very carefully using the specialist pastry cutter.

At this point you should carefully remove the leaf while the dough is still fresh and add a little ball of dough to the back to make it slightly bent and more realistic.

BREAD AND SHELLS

Every region has
a different type of
bread and here are
some of the more
common ones.
With these basic
shapes you can use
your imagination
to create more
advanced projects
like the wreath on
pages 50 and 51.

Shells are pretty
easy to make.
The top ones were
formed with the help
of a toothpick and
the one below
by rolling up a
rectangular strip
of dough.

BOWS

These are all made with very soft and compact dough that can be rolled out thinly. To avoid it drying out while you are working place in aluminium foil.

WREATHS

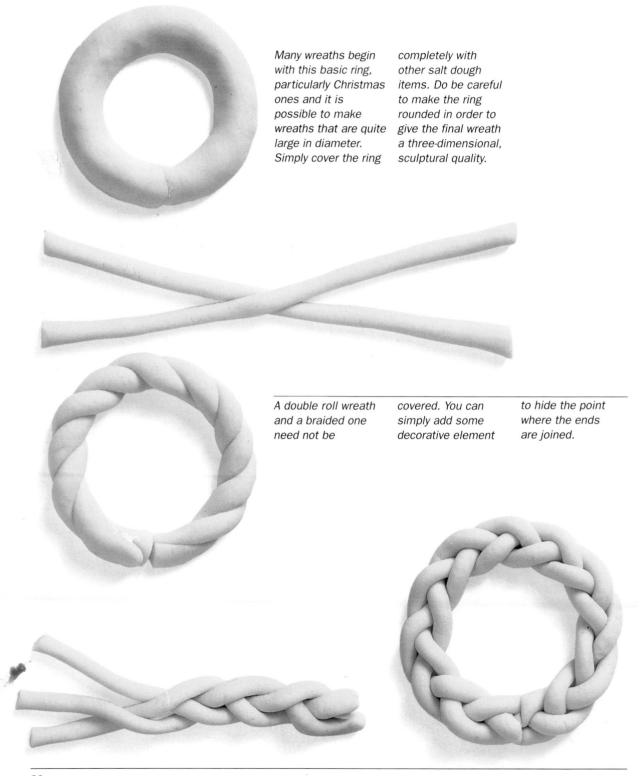

Many wreaths begin with this basic ring, particularly Christmas ones and it is possible to make wreaths that are quite large in diameter. Simply cover the ring completely with other salt dough items. Do be careful to make the ring rounded in order to give the final wreath a three-dimensional, sculptural quality.

A double roll wreath and a braided one need not be covered. You can simply add some decorative element to hide the point where the ends are joined.

If you do not have a frame ready to be decorated you can always make one and it does not have to be perfect! Take a sheet of dough about $\frac{1}{2}$ cm/ $\frac{1}{4}$ in thick and cut out a window. It is a good idea to add metal picture holders to the back while the dough is still fresh.

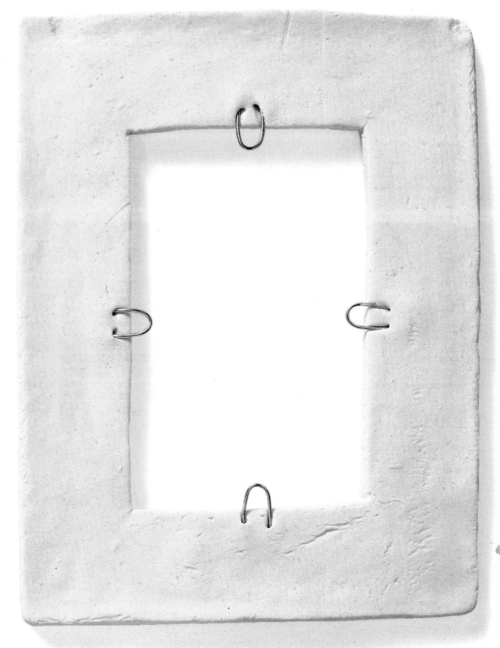

BASKETS

To make a three-dimensional basket all you need to do is cover a bowl or teacup with cellophane wrap. Starting from the centre, cover the entire surface area with twisted dough strips making sure that the strips adhere to each other with the aid of a wet paintbrush. Remove the dough basket from its mould only when the piece is completely dry.

You can also get good results by taking imprints from household objects like this wire mesh to create a woven look.

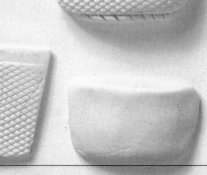

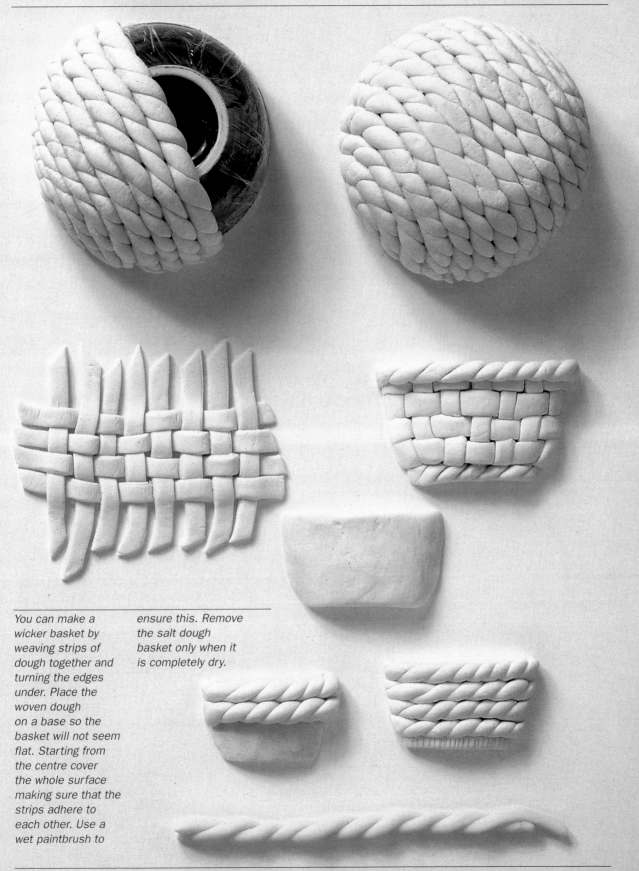

You can make a wicker basket by weaving strips of dough together and turning the edges under. Place the woven dough on a base so the basket will not seem flat. Starting from the centre cover the whole surface making sure that the strips adhere to each other. Use a wet paintbrush to ensure this. Remove the salt dough basket only when it is completely dry.

FOUR ANIMALS

There are no particular rules on how to make the little animals shown here. The proportions are important but above all it's the natural sense of movement that you want to capture in the way you assemble the pieces.

The little bear and rabbit are very alike. Attach lively and pudgy arms and legs to the body. Although they have similar faces and mouths, their ears are different.

The same goes for this little monkey except that the arms and legs are more tapered and the proportions of the face are different.

This goose is very simple to make. The only thing you have to remember is to roll the dough in your fingers to make a long neck.

HOW TO
MAKE WORDS

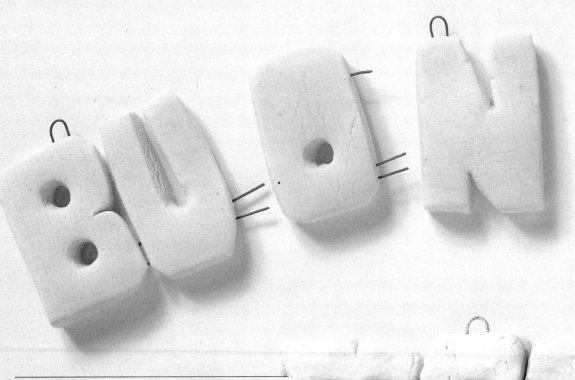

The best way of course is to use letter-shaped pastry cutters but the choices are rather limited and it can be quite expensive. From a flat sheet of dough about 1cm/$\frac{1}{2}$ in thick, carve out simple letters using a knife or a specialist pastry cutter. The easier the graphic style the better. The letters are attached to each other by toothpicks or wire. To hang the letters add bent wire hooks while the dough is fresh.

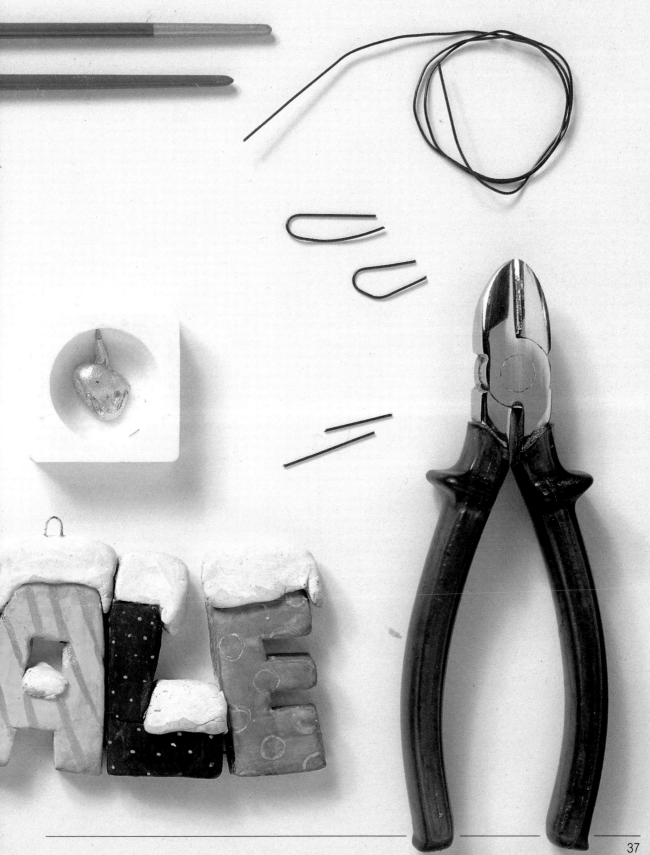

CHRISTMAS
TIME

CHRISTMAS TREES

Christmas time is a magical time for those who like working with salt dough; you can be as creative as you like with tremendous results. You can make presents for friends and relatives with Christmas motifs that lend themselves to a wealth of festive decorations. It could be a nativity scene that takes hours to complete or a simple gold star made with a pastry cutter; it does not matter because whatever it is you make it will be special and individual.

RED AND GREEN CHRISTMAS TREE

The traditional colours of red and green give this tree a very festive quality. Alternating red and green hearts are glued to a gold cord to make a long chain that is then wound around the tree.

This dark green wreath is decorated with salt dough stars and a bright red ribbon.

These hearts were cut from a 1cm/ $\frac{1}{2}$ in thick sheet of dough and they can be completely plain, varied in size or have some decoration. The little balls on the third heart were imprinted with a straw.

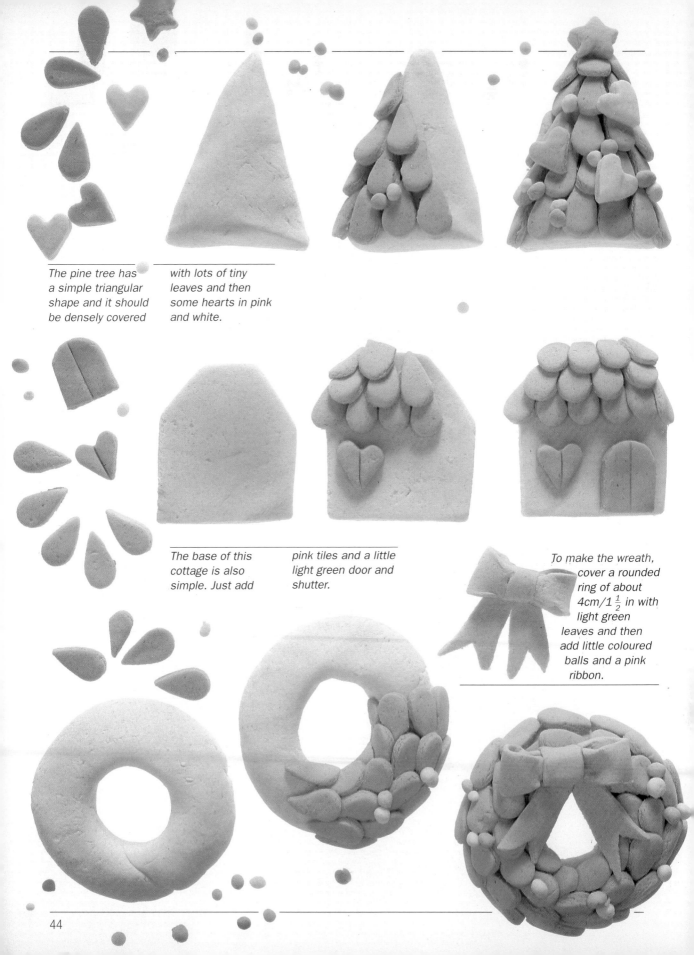

The pine tree has a simple triangular shape and it should be densely covered with lots of tiny leaves and then some hearts in pink and white.

The base of this cottage is also simple. Just add pink tiles and a little light green door and shutter.

To make the wreath, cover a rounded ring of about 4cm/1 $\frac{1}{2}$ in with light green leaves and then add little coloured balls and a pink ribbon.

PASTEL CHRISTMAS TREE

This evergreen tree has been decorated in non-traditional colours but the end result is very pretty. It has been adorned with little dough houses, trees and wreaths in pale pink and green. The decorations and ribbons have been attached to the tree with a hot glue gun.

CHRISTMAS TREE WITH STARS

Ivory and gold are the basic colours of this tree. The stars were cut using pastry cutters of various sizes. They have been covered in gold paint or have been left natural giving a pretty coordinated look to the tree. They have been attached to this artificial evergreen tree with a hot glue gun.

To make open-centred stars, you should roll a 1cm/$\frac{1}{2}$ in sheet of dough and cut out a large star and then cut out a smaller one within it using two appropriately-sized pastry cutters.

CHRISTMAS GARLANDS

Pine trees are easily cut out from a sheet of green dough, then make small holes in the sides with a straw in order to tie the pieces together with a thin green ribbon.

The little wreaths can also be cut from a sheet of green dough and then covered with little balls and stars in festive colours.

Finally you should add a bright red ribbon and remember to make the little holes to tie the pieces together.

These are the same hearts which were tied to the red and green Christmas tree. You can use them to decorate pieces of furniture, a window or a fireplace. The hearts have been made using a pastry cutter.

These Santas with their jolly faces have been tied between the green wreaths. Once again, remember the ribbon holes.

NATURAL WREATHS

Wreaths left uncoloured are enchanting because they remind you of freshly baked bread. Charming little bears have been added to this wreath of apples and leaves to make an unusual, attractive combination.

This dense wreath of grapes has been moulded on to the usual base ring. It is quite big but not very difficult to create and it looks very impressive.

ANGEL WREATH

This beautiful festive wreath of artificial evergreen material was purchased in a special craft shop. The angels have been made separately in a natural dough with lots of painted gold decoration like the stars you see here. Attach the pieces to the wreath with a hot glue gun.

TWO HEARTS

Look for hearts made from natural material in special craft shops; add one or two coloured decorations and they become beautiful gifts. One of the hearts was made with dried evergreen material and the other from twigs. The little apples on the first and lemons and oranges on the second were moulded directly on to the wreaths. In case they do not adhere, once dry use some hot glue. Choosing your ribbon colour is important in bringing the piece together and a touch of gold will make it delightfully festive.

54

CHRISTMAS PRESENT DECORATIONS

These red and green Christmas packages make the present inside even more special. To make the pine tree just squeeze the dough through a piping bag. The initialled heart (with garlic press dough thread) is surrounded by what looks like fabric. Actually it is a sheet of dough that has been pressed very thinly between two sheets of cellophane and then gently folded.

Make the stars with tiny pastry cutters and they can be dotted all over Christmas packages using glue.

This decoration looks like a Tyrolean ribbon: make little roses (three petals around a little ball) and cut out some leaves. Often the simplest ideas are the best!

CHRISTMAS WISHES FROM AROUND THE WORLD

"Merry Christmas" is the wish people give each other in the UK; all around the world it's customary to exchange Christmas greetings. Here is an opportunity to do just that with foreign friends from all over the world with these examples of writing in dough, indulging in various whims of decoration.

On the letters forming Merry Christmas festive objects have been moulded: stars, candy canes, hearts, trees, angels and bows which have all been painted in gold and other bright colours.

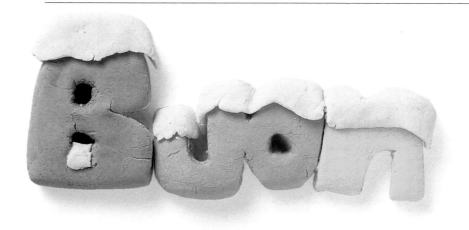

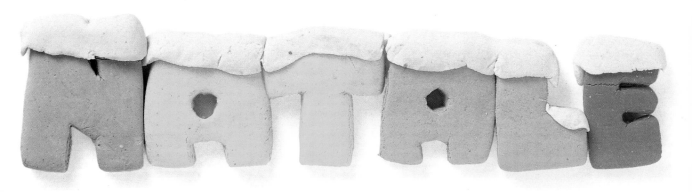

Alternating red and green dough letters form a German "Fröhe Weihnachten" with the addition of gold and hearts. Such long words require lots of toothpicks or wire reinforcements to insure they do not fall apart.

The Spanish "Buenas Navidades" begins with leaves and berries and is written in rolls of green dough.

The greeting in French, "Joyeux Noël", has been painted all over in red and green *with an added touch of gold to make it special for Christmas.*

NATIVITY SCENE

This is a rural nativity scene that is quite demanding but very rewarding to make. Start with a wooden board, make dough the colour of wood and create a framework in which to put the characters of the nativity as well as other objects. Coloured dough was mostly used for this scene except for some small details which were painted.

NATURAL NATIVITY SCENE

The same nativity scene can be approached in two ways: in natural dough as seen here or brightly-coloured. This ivory version is simpler and perhaps more elegant.

PAINTED NATIVITY SCENE

If you want a more traditional scene all you have to do is paint the pieces using plenty of gold for the robes of the three wise men. It is a good idea to go over all the pieces with some fine-grade sand paper before painting in order to smooth off any imperfections.

To make the characters stand upright, model the bodies with a bit of wire reinforcement and bake them in the oven. Then add the head, arms, robes and let the piece dry.

Painting the figures should be done very delicately in order to avoid smears and you should be careful to leave no unpainted spots.

TABLE DECORATION

The Christmas table should look sumptuous and this is why an abundance of gold is a good idea. So that the fruit doesn't look monotonous, it is pretty to add a second gold colour.

Alice

Make a centrepiece by filling a small wooden container with dough. Then add your dough objects, remembering to add the candles at the beginning. In order to avoid uneven candle holes during the drying period, place aluminium foil cups in them moulded round the base of your chosen candles, before putting the piece in the oven.

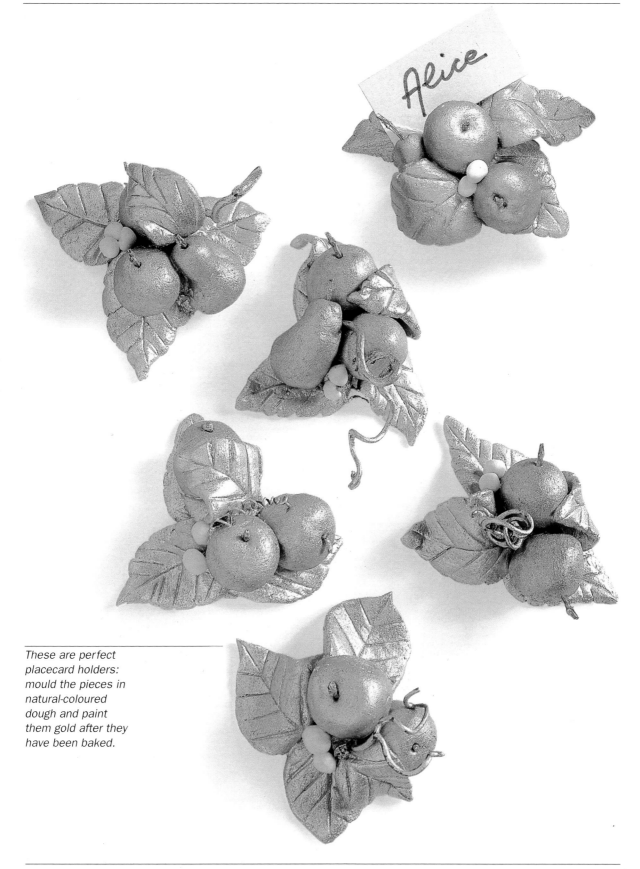

These are perfect placecard holders: mould the pieces in natural-coloured dough and paint them gold after they have been baked.

IDEAS
FOR SPECIAL
OCCASIONS

PATCHWORK INSPIRATIONS

With this series of projects the secret lies in the painting, which must be meticulous and precise so as to imitate the fabrics used for patchwork quilts.

To make the piece on the previous page, cut six squares from a sheet of dough $\frac{1}{2}$ cm/$\frac{1}{4}$ in thick and in each press the shape of a heart with a pastry cutter without quite cutting through the dough. Decorate each piece imitating patchwork fabric and stick together with a hot glue gun.

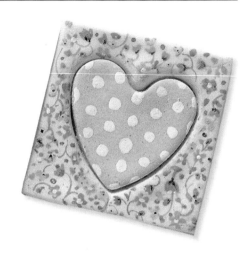

Take a simple, small, wooden frame (or make one following the instructions on page 31) and cover it with dough pieces, some of which are already coloured and some natural. Try to create a stuffed or puffy effect. Finish off by painting on delicate decorations in pastel.

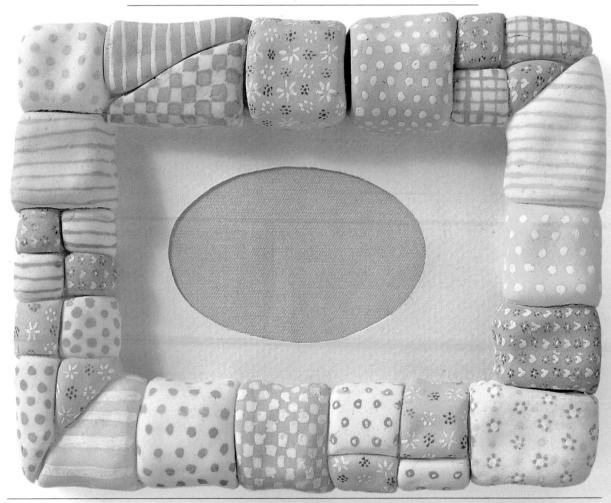

This looks just like a plaited fabric wreath about 30cm/15in in diameter with a big ribbon. Take three long rolls of coloured dough and plait them together adding the dough ribbon at the point where the ends meet. Then paint delicate, print-like designs.

FRAME WITH HEARTS

Inside this unpainted wooden frame are several hearts hung by satin ribbons. Each one has been made with great attention to detail.

To create this scalloped lace heart, simply carve the design using a toothpick.

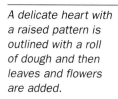

A delicate heart with a raised pattern is outlined with a roll of dough and then leaves and flowers are added.

Long rolls of dough shape this simple but elegant heart.

To make this basket-weave heart, first weave the strips of dough and then cut out a heart shape with a pastry cutter.

Cover a heart base
with tiny flowers
to create a most
romantic effect.

The most delicate
flowers and leaves
make this heart a
true labour of love.

To create a dimpled
effect this dough
heart has been
pressed on to a
cheese grater.

A frilled border
enriches this simple
heart decorated with
flowers using a
toothpick.

WALL SAMPLER

This panel is like a cross stitch sampler with repeated designs. Samplers are an inexhaustible source of ideas for those wanting to have fun with dough. The whole design is great fun but each of the pieces herein can be given as individual presents.

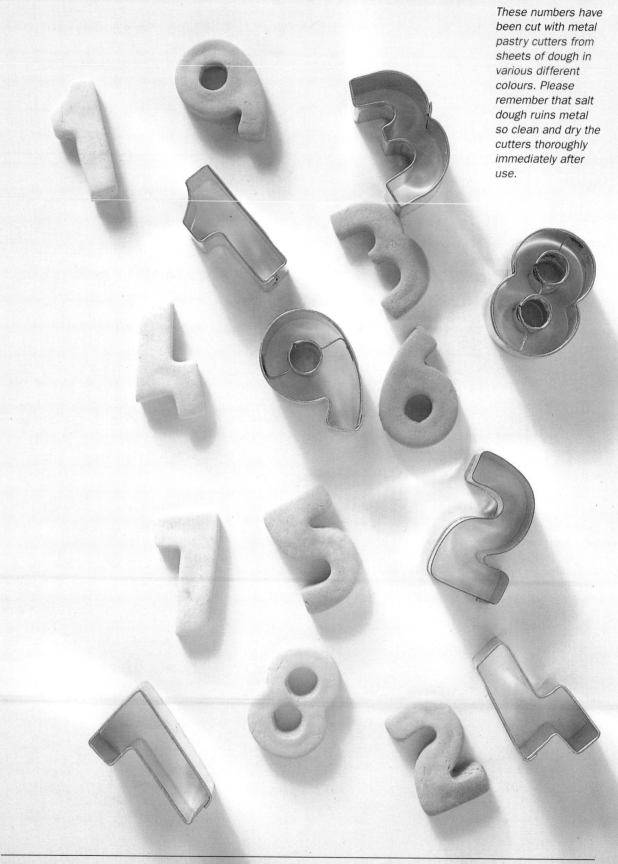

These numbers have been cut with metal pastry cutters from sheets of dough in various different colours. Please remember that salt dough ruins metal so clean and dry the cutters thoroughly immediately after use.

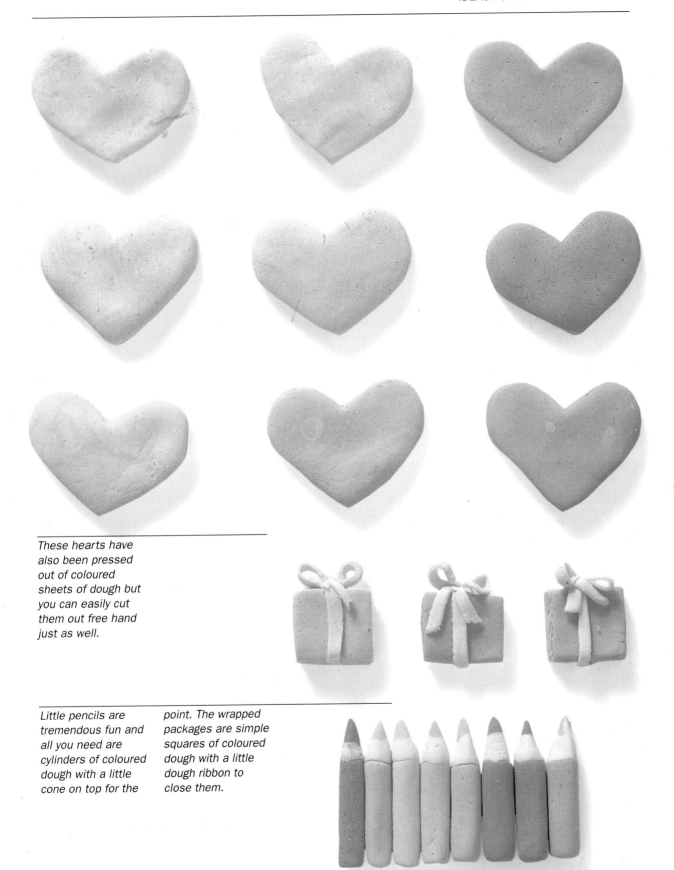

These hearts have also been pressed out of coloured sheets of dough but you can easily cut them out free hand just as well.

Little pencils are tremendous fun and all you need are cylinders of coloured dough with a little cone on top for the point. The wrapped packages are simple squares of coloured dough with a little dough ribbon to close them.

Little pastry cutters have been used to create the stars, and the moon and cloud were modelled by hand.

Make this kite with four different coloured triangles of dough, cut with a knife or specialist pastry cutter and then stick together.

Follow the instructions on page 35 to make these charming geese.

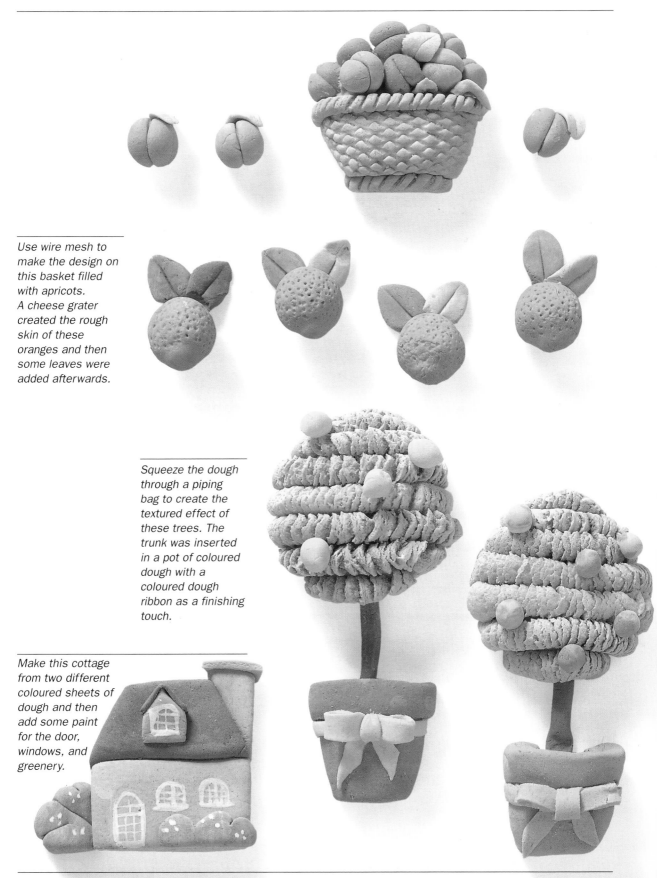

Use wire mesh to make the design on this basket filled with apricots. A cheese grater created the rough skin of these oranges and then some leaves were added afterwards.

Squeeze the dough through a piping bag to create the textured effect of these trees. The trunk was inserted in a pot of coloured dough with a coloured dough ribbon as a finishing touch.

Make this cottage from two different coloured sheets of dough and then add some paint for the door, windows, and greenery.

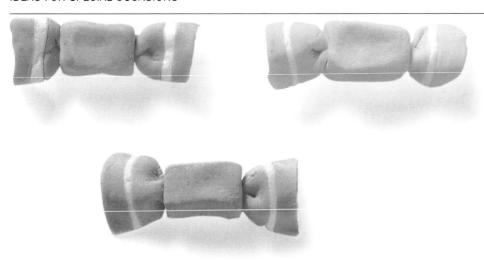

Adding some cubes of dough, tucked in at the ends, to these rectangles will create perfect sweets.

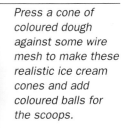

Press a cone of coloured dough against some wire mesh to make these realistic ice cream cones and add coloured balls for the scoops.

Press a toothpick vertically along the side of these coloured cones to make the folds and add a handle with a small ribbon to create these colourful umbrellas.

Mould lots of tiny flowers in different colours and add them to a garland base. Finish off this piece with two blue ribbons.

These little roses are only 1cm/$\frac{1}{2}$ in wide and they need to be made with a lot of care. See page 22 for the technique.

So easy to make, these leaves are unusual because of their autumn colours.

Squeezed through a piping bag, these delicate wreaths are then decorated with tiny flowers and a ribbon.

WOODLAND TABLE DECORATIONS

A host of wild fruit including strawberries, blueberries and blackberries have been made with great care and this stunning combination will liven up any table setting.

Use a wooden container as the base for this centrepiece and fill it with dough. Then add the dough decorations that you have created separately remembering to leave spaces for two candles. Wrap the candle bases in aluminium foil and insert them to make sure the holes remain the right shape. Leave the aluminium foil in place until the piece is completely dry. Choose your candles and ribbons to go with the dough colours that you use.

As far as placecard holders go, these are real masterpieces. Mould one of the base leaves upright at the back in order to make a slot for the card.

For this centrepiece make a twisted oval base using natural-coloured dough and roll a thin green strip of dough round it upon which to place the wild flowers and berries.

FLOWER PLACECARD HOLDERS

Hydrangeas are the subject of these placecard holders. Mould three round veiny leaves and remember to make one slightly raised to hold the placecard. Then cover a green dough ball with little pink or white flowers and place it in the centre of the leaves.

These sweet little name tags are made with dough daisies and the name can be written with a marker or with strips of dough put through a garlic press.

The ivory colour of natural dough moulded into many pieces on a similar theme, like a rose for example, is perfect for this special day. They are simple and should have very thin petals made from hard dough following the instructions on page 22.

This dough heart base is completely covered in natural-coloured roses with green ribbon in between each one.

A simple oval with the bride's and groom's names is a nice accompaniment to a wedding present. The names can be written with little threads of dough pressed through the garlic press and shaped with the help of a toothpick.

Over a dough frame (see page 31) place a series of natural-coloured dough roses but pay careful attention to choose the right colour cardboard mount for the frame.

For the little sweet bag, green ribbon was chosen to go with lace, ivory ribbon and an ivory natural coloured rose which is attached using a hot glue gun.

EASTER

Pink, light green and bright yellow; these colours work very well for Easter because they are the same as those of primroses, new grass, daffodils, buttercups and tulips. A sunny yellow ribbon completes this spring picture.

Make lots of different kinds of flowers to fill this Easter basket wall decoration but first make the basket base following the instructions on page 32. Then add salt dough eggs in pastel colours and finally flowers and some leaves. To be sure that the composition is not flat, start from a slightly curved base that will give the piece a three-dimensional look when it's finished.

Flower-covered eggs require a bit of patience and skill but they are fun to make and very decorative. First make an egg a little bit smaller than a real one. Cover it completely with the little flowers overlapping each other starting at the bottom of the egg. Here are samples with primroses, violets and forget-me-nots. The eggs should be slightly flattened at the back and then glued on to a picture mount and framed.

This is a demanding but delightful project. After making the basket (see page 32) create a base in the bottom of it with aluminium foil and dough. Then make lifesize eggs and place them in the basket alternating the colours. Fill the spaces between the eggs with daffodils, violets, buttercups and primroses.

GREENGROCER'S SHOP

With dedication, attention to detail and patience this project will bring much satisfaction but it is perhaps not good for beginners. Start with a wooden board surrounded by an inspiring frame. Using techniques from previous sections this must be created in parts that will be put together piece by piece.

MILLINER'S SHOP

The milliner's window is much smaller than the greengrocer's and it is very feminine with use of lots of delicate colours. This ensemble also begins with a piece of plywood as a base and there should be a range of complementing colours in both the background and the objects included.

COUNTRY COTTAGE

The interior of a country cottage is reproduced in just a small space (30 x 20cm/15 x 10in) including all the furniture, utensils, and dishes. The background board works very well as it is in country style and tones in with the furniture.

The stove is little more than a cube of dough with doors, handles, feet and pots added on.

Home sweet home

A little clothes rail with the classic country-style straw hat.

This small cupboard was made from a rectangular sweet box, lined with dough and filled with little dough objects.

To make this bed see pages 142-4. It is 5cm/2 $\frac{1}{2}$ in thick.

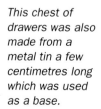

This chest of drawers was also made from a metal tin a few centimetres long which was used as a base.

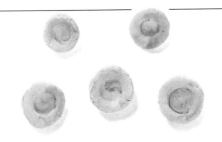

This sideboard was made from a simple shape in a lightish green colour. Using the top of a ballpoint pen, mould the little plates hanging above.

The many little objects that rest on this shelf are all made with natural-coloured dough and then painted with very diluted paint in order to obtain a ceramic effect.

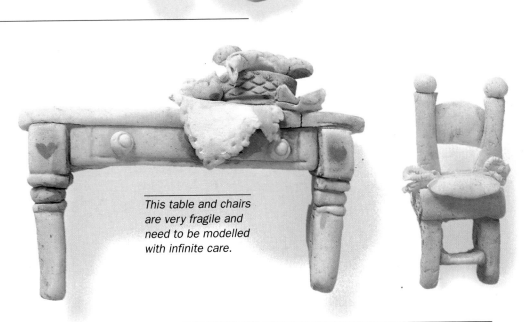

This table and chairs are very fragile and need to be modelled with infinite care.

117

ST VALENTINE'S DAY GIFTS

These are very elegant present decorations for a special St Valentine's day. Using white, blue and red for simple dough shapes will ensure beautiful results.

Here are two examples of name plaques as presents. Sara's is more whimsical while Alex's is simpler.

In this elegant trimming white and blue flowers have been modelled and glued to a red ribbon.

This red rose will be perfect on a white package given to that special someone.

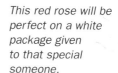

Here are twelve different hearts decorated using straws and imprinted with patterns from everyday kitchen objects that make a perfect gift ... from the heart.

COLOURFUL GIFT-WRAPPING DECORATIONS

A single big rose is enough to complete a fuscia wrapped present.

Here is a series of cleverly wrapped packages using tissue paper in bright colours. The dough decorations were created specially for each gift to make sure the whole parcel looked just right.

A romantic bunch of violets brightens up the lilac-coloured package.

Use a colourful bunch of fruit with a package wrapped in green tones.

Yellow, orange and white daffodils (see page 21 for instructions) look wonderful on an orange parcel.

For Julie's birthday, the idea of adding a name tag decorated with little dough flowers designed with a straw adds a lovely personal touch.

DECORATING
WITH LEAVES

Using the instructions on pages 26-7, it is easy to decorate simple objects with beautiful, realistic dough leaves, transforming them into gifts that will be sure to please.

Resembling herbal collections of the past, you can create this wall hanging using a simple, rustic, wooden frame. Common leaves have been reproduced here: maple, oak, grape vine, beechwood, blackberry, strawberry and raspberry. The veins have been painted in light or dark green and then the finished leaves have been glued on to the cardboard mount.

This picture frame is decorated with vine leaves and has a green checked mount which creates a very pretty surround for a portrait. The leaves were moulded in various shades of green dough with real vine stalks added.

This unfinished wooden box looks just right with natural ivory-coloured dough leaves in various shapes and sizes. Please note in this and other compositions that it is important that the leaves look three-dimensional and a little dough placed underneath them here and there will give that effect.

An old round wooden box is given a new lease on life with natural-coloured dough leaves and a green ribbon.

A TASTE OF THE SEA

Moulding dough
seashells and
starfish is easy,
just follow the
instructions on page
28. For optimum
results use diluted
paint that lets a bit
of the dough's
natural colour show
through.

This picture frame is perfect for a photo taken by the seaside. Make a dough base (see page 31) and cover it with shells and sea life painted in watercolours.

Here is another
frame perfect for a
photo or a little
mirror.

Light paints allow
the natural colour of
the dough to show
through.

MAGNETS

Dough works really well when making refrigerator and bulletin board magnets that are so popular today. In fact, you can create a whole collection of them. Many of the little objects seen in this book are perfect and all you need to do is glue a magnet, that can be found in any hardware shop, to the back of your piece.

GIFTS FOR CHILDREN

SWEETS

Toffees, gumdrops, and other sweets can be moulded from pastel-coloured dough in various shapes and sizes with careful consideration of your colour combinations.

Attach them to a frame (see page 31) and then paint in the details, perhaps adding a blue-grey bow.

The diameter of this wreath is 20cm/10in and it has been moulded on to a curved ring to ensure the three- dimensional look of the sweets that are attached. A pale blue bow creates a beautiful finish.

FOR A NEW BABY

Four charming scenes dedicated to a newborn baby, these will surely bring pleasure to the new mother too. Including the birthdate adds a perfect personal touch.

Make Alice's bed in layers: first the headboard, then the pillow, the sheet and blanket and finally the end of the bed with the child's name. The face and toys should be added at the end.

The whole finished piece should be no more than 6-7cm/3-$3\frac{1}{4}$ in thick. Attach it to the background with a hot glue gun and add some hearts and a ribbon in coloured dough.

This baby girl's summer outfit is pink and white, of course. The sweetest item is the pair of shoes which require real patience and are moulded on the tip of your little finger.

To make Paul's bed follow the instructions on page 143.

The colours this time should be light blue since it is a boy's bed.

For David, born in the winter, there is a snowsuit with a woollen suit, sleeveless sweater, *jumper and dungarees. Do not forget the mittens, hat and scarf.*

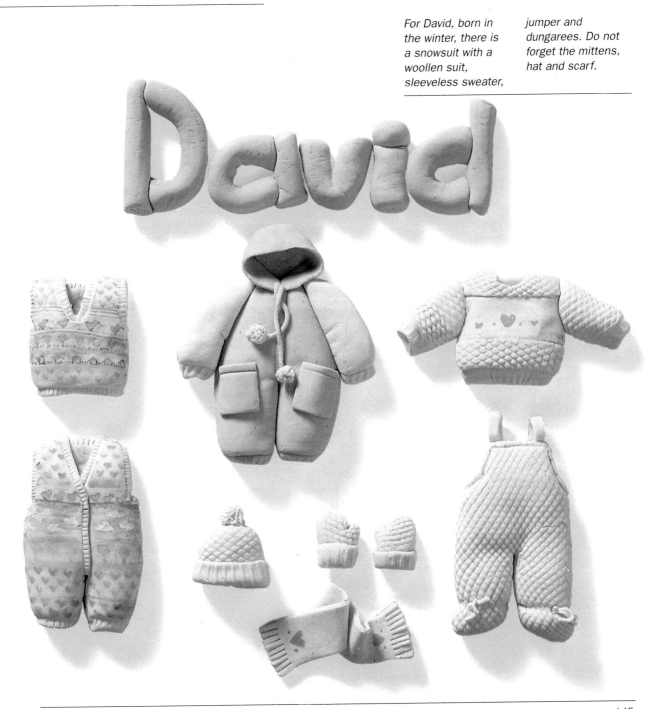

This baby frog with his cheeky face is perfect for a party. The rocking horse is an original idea. Use a garlic press to make the mane and tail.

GIFT-WRAPPING FOR CHILDREN

The heart for Paul is easy. Just put two hearts on top of each other and write the name using dough pushed through a garlic press.

Using coloured dough make the little chick which was taken from the design on the wrapping paper.

LEARNING TO COUNT

These two wall hangings are not just supposed to be educational. With a little imagination they make the perfect decoration for a baby's room. Use coloured dough for all these projects.

The little monkeys are really appealing and it is important that they are modelled in really life-like positions. Small animals and natural objects, carefully made and put together form the counting picture

on the right. Like the wall sampler on page 84, here are many ideas in miniature. They are all easy to copy but the bigger animals are a little more difficult.

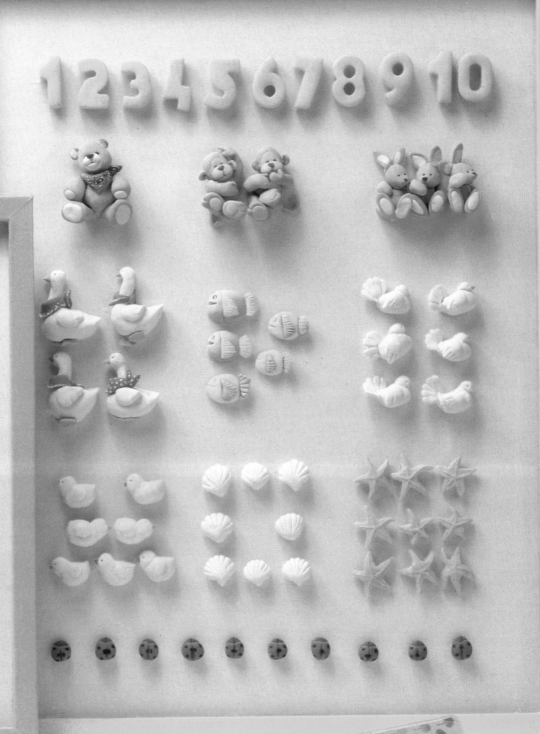

Numbers 1 to 9 are presented by a charming little monkey with an air of fun and cleverness. Once you have practiced with a sample monkey, it is easy to create an infinite number of positions.

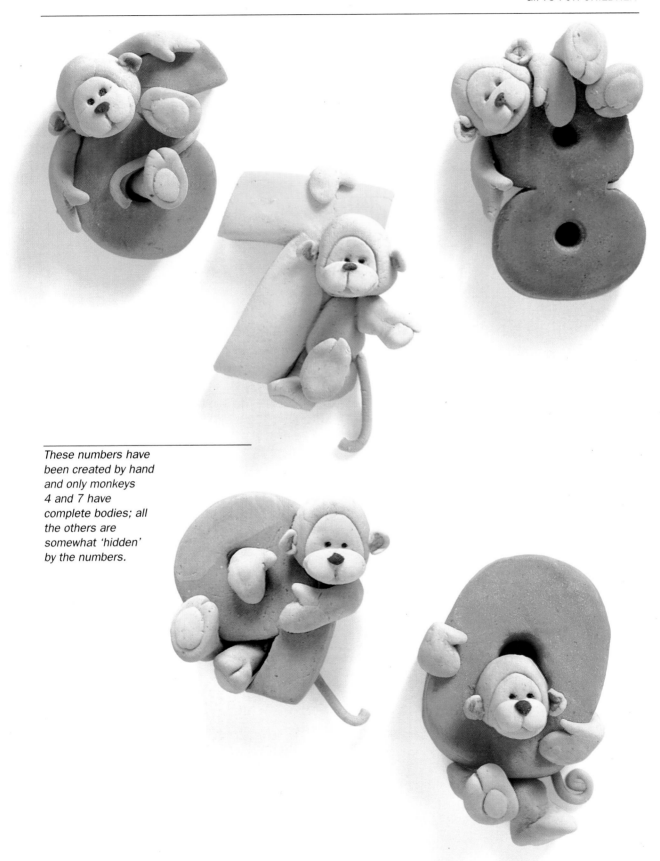

These numbers have
been created by hand
and only monkeys
4 and 7 have
complete bodies; all
the others are
somewhat 'hidden'
by the numbers.

1 *This bear has a handpainted bandanna; be imaginative with the colours you choose.*

2 *These crazy monkeys can be made following instructions on page 35.*

3 *Make these three delightful green bunnies using the instructions on page 35.*

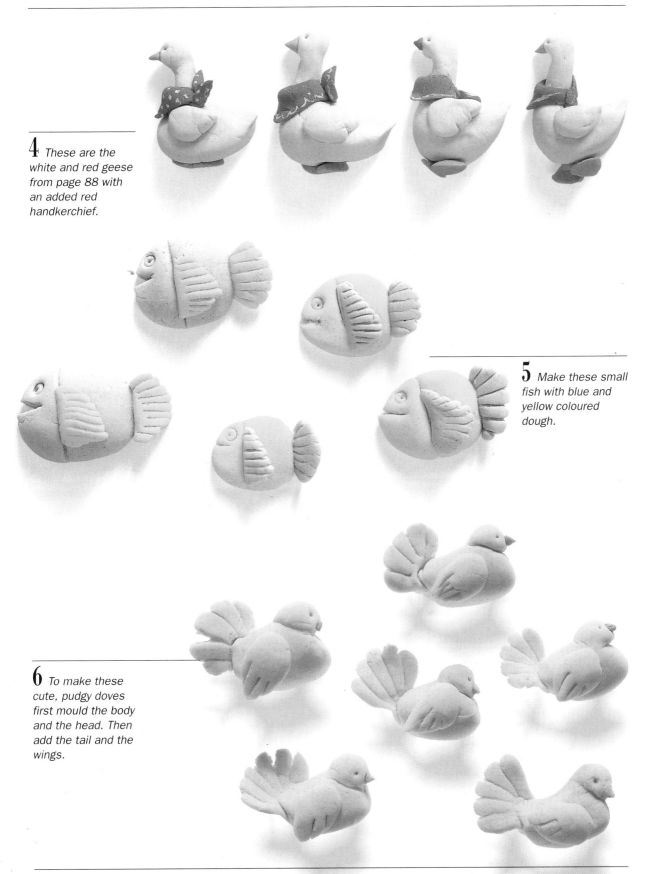

4 *These are the white and red geese from page 88 with an added red handkerchief.*

5 *Make these small fish with blue and yellow coloured dough.*

6 *To make these cute, pudgy doves first mould the body and the head. Then add the tail and the wings.*

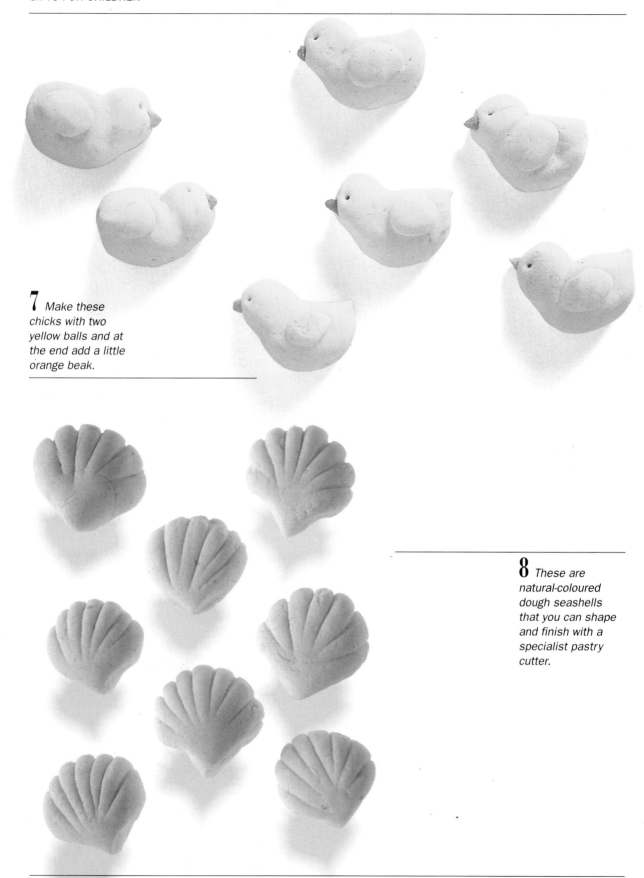

7 *Make these chicks with two yellow balls and at the end add a little orange beak.*

8 *These are natural-coloured dough seashells that you can shape and finish with a specialist pastry cutter.*

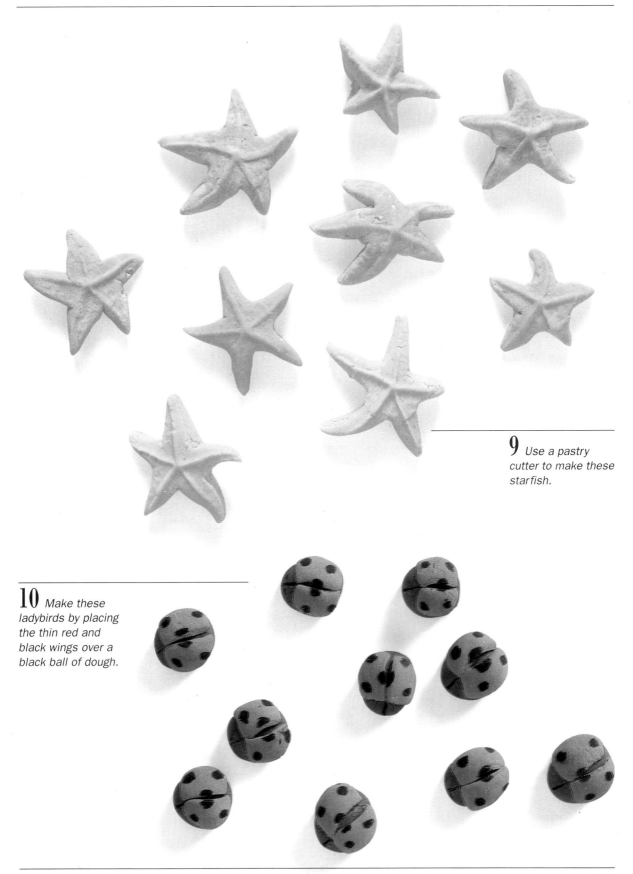

9 *Use a pastry cutter to make these starfish.*

10 *Make these ladybirds by placing the thin red and black wings over a black ball of dough.*

NECKLACES

These necklaces are very easy to make; by experimenting with shapes and colours you can create delightful trinkets. Make the beads in coloured dough and once they are dry go over them with sand paper and varnish them with a gloss finish. Clasps and chains are easy to find in specialist shops.

All children love to make and paint necklaces according to their personal taste. There is no end to the variety you can create.

PROJECT RATINGS

EASY

MEDIUM

ADVANCED

To Luciano, Michele, Matteo

ACKNOWLEDGEMENTS

Luciano, for putting up with salt and flour;
Matteo, so demanding but greatly appreciated for his precious advice;
Michele and Paola, for giving me their time;
My sister Sandra, for taking my place within the family;
Mariuccia Motta, who supported me with her friendship;
Alberto Dell'Orto, of "Linea Verde" (Monza) who gave me natural materials for wreaths and Christmas trees.
The art products producer, APA, of Bologna.
Also my thanks go to Alberto Bertoldi, reliable photographer and a sage and patient master; to Rossana Mungai and the staff at "Benissimo", for making available certain journalistic services; to Cristina Sperandeo, for having believed once again in my salt dough ideas.

Photographs by Alberto Bertoldi
Graphics and paging: Paola Masera and Amelia Verga
Translation: Sally Bloomfield